DEDICATION

To the relentless seekers of knowledge, the curious minds tirelessly decoding the mysteries of algorithms and code. This book is dedicated to you, the coders who embrace the challenges of neural networks with fervor and determination. May these pages serve as stepping stones on your journey, empowering you to unravel the complexities of this dynamic field and craft solutions that shape the future. Your passion fuels the innovation that drives our world forward, and for that, I extend my deepest gratitude and admiration.

The Internet of Things

A Comprehensive Exploration

Benjamin Evans

Copyright © 2024 Benjamin Evans

All rights reserved.

CONTENTS

ACKNOWLEDGMENTS 1
CHAPTER 1 1
Unveiling the Internet of Things (IoT) 1
    1.1 The Dawn of a Connected World - Tracing the Evolution of the Concept and its Transition from Science Fiction to Reality 1
    1.2 Unveiling the "Things" in IoT - Exploring the Vast Array of Devices that Make Up the Interconnected Ecosystem 4
    1.3 Understanding the "Internet" of Things - Diving into Communication Protocols, Data Exchange, and Network Infrastructure. 6
    1.4 The Ripple Effect of IoT - Examining the Impact of IoT on Different Aspects of Life, from Industries to Individuals 8
CHAPTER 2 11
The Foundations of IoT 11
    2.1 The Power of Perception: Sensors & Data Acquisition 11
    2.2 The Language of Machines: Communication Protocols 14
    2.3 Processing Power: From Microcontrollers to the Cloud 16
    2.4 Data: The Lifeblood of IoT 17
CHAPTER 3 20
A Symphony of Smart Devices 20
    3.1 The Smart Home Orchestra: Automating Your Living Space 20
    3.2 Wearables: Transforming Wellness on Your Wrist 22
    3.3 Smart Cities: Building the Future, Today 23
    3.4 Industrial Symphony: Revolutionizing Manufacturing with IoT 25
CHAPTER 4 28
Unlocking the Power of IoT Data 28
    4.1 Data Collection & Analytics: From Raw Data to Valuable Insights. 28
    4.2 Big Data & Machine Learning: Supercharging Decision-Making.... 30
    4.3 Data Visualization: Transforming Numbers into Actionable Stories... 32
    4.4 Security & Privacy: Protecting the Data Symphony 33

CHAPTER 5 .... **36**

IoT Revolutionizing Industries **36**

    5.1 Retail Revolution: Personalized Shopping Experiences 36

    5.2 Cultivating the Future: Precision Farming with IoT 38

    5.3 Healthcare Transformed: Remote Patient Monitoring & Data-Driven Care 39

    5.4 Transportation Evolved: Connected Vehicles for a Safer Journey .. 40

CHAPTER 6 .... **43**

Glimpsing the Future: Emerging Trends & Innovations **43**

    6.1 Artificial Intelligence (AI) & IoT: A Match Made in Tech Heaven 43

    6.2 Blockchain & IoT: Building Trust in a Connected World 45

    6.3 The Rise of Edge Computing: Processing Power Closer to the Source 46

    6.4 The Internet of Everything (IoE): Connecting Everything, Everywhere 48

CHAPTER 7 .... **51**

The Societal Impact of IoT **51**

    7.1 Smart Cities & Sustainable Living: Building a Greener Future 51

    7.2 Connected Communities & Improved Public Services 53

    7.3 The Future of Work: Automation & The Changing Landscape 54

    7.4 Ethical Considerations: Privacy, Security, and Bias 55

CHAPTER 8 .... **57**

Securing the Future of IoT **57**

    8.1 Cybersecurity Threats in the IoT Landscape 57

    8.2 Building Secure IoT Systems: Best Practices and Considerations ... 58

    8.3 The Role of Regulations and Standards 60

    8.4 Building a Culture of Cybersecurity 60

CHAPTER 9 .... **63**

The Road Ahead: Challenges and Opportunities **63**

    9.1 Interoperability and Standardization: Ensuring Compatibility 63

    9.2 Scalability and Sustainability: Managing Growth and Environmental Impact 65

    9.3 The Digital Divide and Accessibility: Bridging the Gap 66

    9.4 The Future of Human-Machine Interaction: Collaboration and

    Co-evolution...67
CHAPTER 10...**69**
The Interconnected Future Awaits..**69**
    10.1 A Recap: The Power and Potential of IoT....................... 69
    10.2 A Call to Action: Embracing a Responsible Future.........................70
    10.3 Looking Ahead: A Glimpse into the Evolving Landscape.............. 71
    10.4 A Final Word: The Journey Begins Here........................ 73

ACKNOWLEDGMENTS

I would like to extend my sincere gratitude to all those who have contributed to the realization of this book. First and foremost, I am indebted to my family for their unwavering support and encouragement throughout this endeavor. Their love and understanding have been my anchor in the stormy seas of writing.

I am deeply thankful to the experts whose guidance and insights have illuminated my path and enriched the content of this book. Their mentorship has been invaluable in shaping my understanding and refining my ideas.

I also extend my appreciation to those whose constructive feedback and insightful suggestions have helped polish this work to its finest form.

Furthermore, I am grateful to the countless individuals whose research, publications, and contributions have paved the way for the insights shared in these pages.

Last but not least, I express my heartfelt appreciation to the readers who embark on this journey with me. Your curiosity and engagement breathe life into these words, and it is for you that this book exists.

Thank you all for being part of this remarkable journey.

CHAPTER 1

Unveiling the Internet of Things (IoT)

1.1 The Dawn of a Connected World - Tracing the Evolution of the Concept and its Transition from Science Fiction to Reality

The idea of interconnected devices has captivated imaginations for decades, finding its roots in science fiction stories that depicted a future where machines seamlessly communicate and collaborate. While the concept may have seemed fantastical in the past, the Internet of Things (IoT) has become a rapidly growing reality.

The evolution of IoT can be traced back to the early days of the internet itself. The dream of connecting everyday objects to a network emerged alongside the development of communication protocols and miniaturized computing power. Pioneering concepts like ubiquitous computing and machine-to-machine (M2M) communication laid the groundwork for the interconnected world we see today.

The true dawn of the IoT era can be pinpointed to the convergence of several key factors:

- **The Rise of the Internet:** The widespread adoption of the internet provided the fundamental infrastructure for connecting devices across vast distances. The internet's global reach and established protocols laid the foundation for seamless communication between various "things."
- **Advancements in Sensor Technology:** The miniaturization and cost reduction of sensors made it possible to equip everyday objects with the ability to collect data about their environment. These sensors, ranging from temperature and motion detectors to image and audio sensors, became the eyes and ears of the IoT revolution.
- **Increased Processing Power:** The exponential

growth of computing power allowed for the development of microcontrollers and embedded systems capable of processing sensor data and facilitating communication with the internet. These advancements in processing power enabled devices to become more than just data collectors; they could analyze and act upon the information they gathered.

- **Wireless Connectivity:** The rise of wireless technologies like Wi-Fi, Bluetooth, and Low-Power Wide-Area Networks (LPWAN) made it possible for devices to connect to the internet without the need for cumbersome cables. This seamless connectivity removed a major barrier to widespread IoT adoption.

Today, the Internet of Things is no longer a futuristic concept but a tangible reality. From smart homes and wearables to connected vehicles and industrial machinery, billions of devices are now part of a vast, interconnected network.

1.2 Unveiling the "Things" in IoT - Exploring the Vast Array of Devices that Make Up the Interconnected Ecosystem

The "Things" in IoT encompass a diverse range of everyday objects transformed into intelligent devices through the integration of sensors, processors, and communication capabilities. Here are some key categories:

- **Smart Home Devices:** These include thermostats, lighting systems, appliances, security cameras, and doorbells. Smart home devices can be controlled remotely, automate tasks, and provide valuable insights into energy consumption and home security.

- **Wearables:** Smartwatches, fitness trackers, and health monitors are prominent examples of wearables. These devices collect data on your activity level, heart rate, sleep patterns, and other health metrics, empowering individuals to take a more proactive approach to their well-being.

- **Connected Cars:** Vehicles are becoming

increasingly connected, equipped with sensors for monitoring engine performance, tire pressure, and other parameters. Advanced connected cars can integrate with traffic management systems, offer advanced navigation features, and even pave the way for self-driving capabilities.

- **Industrial IoT (IIoT) Devices:** Factories, warehouses, and production lines are leveraging IIoT devices for predictive maintenance, real-time monitoring of production processes, and improved operational efficiency. Sensors can monitor equipment health, identify potential failures before they occur, and optimize resource utilization.

- **Smart City Infrastructure:** Traffic lights, parking meters, waste bins, and environmental monitoring systems are all becoming connected in smart cities. This allows for real-time data collection, enabling authorities to optimize traffic flow, improve waste management, and create a more sustainable urban environment.

This list is far from exhaustive, and the range of devices encompassed by the IoT continues to expand rapidly. From smart agricultural sensors to connected medical devices, the possibilities are seemingly endless.

1.3 Understanding the "Internet" of Things - Diving into Communication Protocols, Data Exchange, and Network Infrastructure

The "internet" in IoT refers to the network infrastructure that connects these devices and enables them to communicate and exchange data. This communication relies on several key elements:

- **Communication Protocols:** These protocols define the language devices use to speak to each other. Common protocols in IoT include Wi-Fi, Bluetooth, Zigbee, and cellular networks. Each protocol has its own strengths and weaknesses, making the choice dependent on factors like range, power consumption, and data transmission speed.

- **Connectivity Options:** Devices can connect to the internet through various methods depending on their capabilities and application. Traditional Wi-Fi and cellular networks offer high bandwidth but may not be suitable for all devices due to power limitations. Low-Power Wide-Area Networks (LPWAN) are gaining traction as they offer long-range communication with low power consumption, making them ideal for battery-powered sensors.

- **Data Exchange:** Once connected, devices can exchange data with each other and with cloud platforms. This data exchange can be one-way (sensors sending data to a central server) or two-way (devices receiving commands or instructions based on collected data).

- **Network Infrastructure:** The data collected by IoT devices needs to be transported and stored. The network infrastructure for IoT can be complex, often involving a combination of local networks, gateways, and cloud platforms. Local networks connect devices within a specific location, like a home or a factory. Gateways act as translators, converting data from various protocols into a format compatible with the cloud platform. Cloud platforms provide a central location for storing, managing, and analyzing the vast amounts of data generated by IoT devices.

1.4 The Ripple Effect of IoT - Examining the Impact of IoT on Different Aspects of Life, from Industries to Individuals

The impact of IoT is far-reaching and extends across various spheres of our lives. Here are some key areas where IoT is making its mark:

- **Industries:** Manufacturing, logistics, agriculture, and healthcare are just a few of the industries benefiting from IoT. Predictive maintenance, real-time process optimization, and data-driven decision making are leading to increased efficiency, cost savings, and improved product quality.

- **Smart Cities:** IoT is transforming urban environments into smart cities. Connected infrastructure allows for better traffic management, improved waste collection, and real-time environmental monitoring. This paves the way for more sustainable and efficient cities.

- **Homes and Buildings:** Smart homes offer convenience, automation, and enhanced security. Smart buildings can optimize energy consumption and provide a more comfortable and controlled environment for occupants.

- **Individuals:** Wearables and other connected devices empower individuals to take charge of their health and well-being. Real-time health data can provide insights into activity levels, sleep patterns, and potential health concerns.

- **Retail and Consumer Goods:** Retailers are leveraging IoT to improve inventory management, personalize customer experiences, and optimize store operations. Connected products can provide valuable data on usage patterns and consumer behavior.

However, the impact of IoT is not without its challenges. Security vulnerabilities, privacy concerns, and the potential for job displacement due to automation are some of the aspects that need careful consideration and responsible development.

The Internet of Things has ushered in a new era of interconnectedness. As devices become more intelligent and communication networks become more robust, the possibilities for innovation and transformation are limitless. Understanding the core concepts of IoT, the vast array of "things" it encompasses, and the underlying infrastructure that enables communication and data exchange is crucial to navigate this exciting and ever-evolving landscape.

CHAPTER 2

The Foundations of IoT

The Internet of Things (IoT) thrives on a delicate balance between physical and digital worlds. Sensors act as the eyes and ears of this ecosystem, collecting data about the environment. This data is then processed, communicated, and analyzed to generate insights and enable intelligent automation.

2.1 The Power of Perception: Sensors & Data Acquisition

Sensors are the cornerstone of data acquisition in IoT. They act as the bridge between the physical world and the digital realm, translating physical phenomena into electrical signals that can be processed by devices.

Here's a breakdown of different types of sensors used in IoT:

- **Environmental Sensors:** These sensors measure various aspects of the surrounding environment, including:

  - **Temperature sensors:** Monitor air and liquid temperatures, crucial for smart thermostats, climate control systems, and industrial process monitoring.
  - **Humidity sensors:** Measure moisture levels in the air, important for agricultural applications, building automation, and weather monitoring.
  - **Pressure sensors:** Detect changes in pressure, used in appliances like pressure cookers, air conditioners, and vehicle tire pressure monitoring systems.
  - **Light sensors:** Detect light levels, enabling automatic lighting control in homes and buildings, and playing a role in smart agriculture for optimizing plant growth.

- **Air quality sensors:** Monitor pollutants and other components in the air, crucial for improving indoor air quality and environmental monitoring.
- **Biometric Sensors:** These sensors collect data related to a person's biological characteristics, including:

  - **Heart rate sensors:** Monitor heart rate, vital for fitness trackers, wearables, and healthcare applications.
  - **Fingerprints sensors:** Used for secure authentication in smartphones, access control systems, and secure payments.
  - **Facial recognition sensors:** Employed for security applications, access control, and personalized marketing experiences.
  - **Motion sensors:** Detect movement and occupancy, used for security systems, smart lighting control, and automated gestures in

gaming or entertainment.

This is not an exhaustive list, and new sensor technologies are constantly emerging. The choice of sensor depends on the specific application and the type of data needed. Factors like accuracy, power consumption, and cost all influence the selection process.

2.2 The Language of Machines: Communication Protocols

Once sensors have collected data, devices need to communicate with each other and with cloud platforms. This communication relies on standardized protocols, which act as a common language for machines. Here are some key communication protocols used in IoT:

- **Wi-Fi:** Offers high bandwidth connectivity for devices with a reliable power source, commonly used in smart home devices like thermostats and entertainment systems.
- **Bluetooth:** Provides short-range, low-power

communication, ideal for wearables, fitness trackers, and connecting devices to smartphones.

- **Zigbee:** A low-power mesh networking protocol well-suited for large-scale deployments in smart homes and building automation systems.
- **Cellular Networks:** Offer wide area coverage and high data transfer rates, used for connected vehicles, industrial applications, and remote monitoring systems.
- **Low-Power Wide-Area Networks (LPWAN):** These protocols are gaining traction as they provide long-range connectivity with low power consumption, making them ideal for battery-powered sensors in smart agriculture, asset tracking, and environmental monitoring.

The choice of protocol depends on factors like data transmission speed, range, power consumption, and cost. Some devices may even utilize multiple protocols depending on the communication needs.

2.3 Processing Power: From Microcontrollers to the Cloud

The raw data collected by sensors needs to be processed to extract meaning and enable intelligent actions. Processing power in IoT can be deployed at three main levels:

- **Device Level:** Microcontrollers are small, low-power computers embedded within IoT devices. They can perform basic processing tasks like filtering sensor data, making simple decisions, and communicating with other devices using chosen protocols.
- **Edge Computing:** Edge computing involves processing data closer to the source of collection, on devices like gateways or edge servers. This reduces latency (delay) in data processing and can be beneficial for applications requiring real-time decisions or where internet connectivity may be limited.
- **Cloud Computing:** Cloud platforms offer powerful

processing capabilities for complex data analysis and storage. IoT devices can send data to the cloud for advanced analytics, machine learning, and integration with other systems.

2.4 Data: The Lifeblood of IoT

The vast amount of data generated by IoT devices is its lifeblood. However, managing this data effectively is crucial. Here are some key aspects of data management in the context of IoT:

- **Data Storage:** Cloud platforms are a popular choice for storing large volumes of IoT data. However, depending on the sensitivity of the data or the need for real-time access, on-premise storage solutions or edge devices with local storage capabilities may also be utilized.
- **Data Management:** Strategies are needed to organize, filter, and analyze the data. This may involve data cleansing to remove errors and

inconsistencies, and data transformation to prepare it for analysis.

- **Data Security:** Securing IoT data is paramount, as it can be sensitive and vulnerable to cyberattacks. Encryption, access controls, and secure communication protocols are essential for protecting data privacy and integrity.

The ever-growing volume of data generated by IoT devices presents both opportunities and challenges. Effective data management practices are crucial to ensure the security, usability, and value of this valuable resource.

Sensors, communication protocols, processing power, and data management form the core foundations of the IoT ecosystem. Understanding these building blocks is essential for anyone who wants to delve deeper into the world of connected devices and unlock the potential of this transformative technology. By harnessing the power of perception, establishing a common language for machines, distributing processing capabilities strategically, and managing the lifeblood of data effectively, the possibilities for innovation and intelligent automation in the world of IoT are limitless.

CHAPTER 3

A Symphony of Smart Devices

The Internet of Things (IoT) isn't just about technology; it's about creating a symphony of connected devices that work together to improve our lives.

3.1 The Smart Home Orchestra: Automating Your Living Space

Imagine a home that anticipates your needs and responds seamlessly. This is the promise of the smart home, where a diverse range of connected devices work in concert to enhance comfort, security, and convenience. Here are some key players in the smart home orchestra:

- **Smart Appliances:** Ovens that preheat on command, refrigerators that monitor inventory, and washing machines that send notifications when your laundry is done – these are just a few examples of smart appliances. They can be controlled remotely, integrate with other smart home devices, and even optimize energy consumption.

- **Smart Thermostats:** Learning thermostats automatically adjust to your preferences and schedule, ensuring a comfortable living environment while saving energy. They can be controlled remotely, allowing you to adjust the temperature before you arrive home.

- **Smart Lighting Systems:** Transform your home's ambiance with smart lights. Dim the lights for movie night, schedule them to turn on at sunset, or even control them with your voice. Smart lighting systems can also integrate with motion sensors for added security and convenience.

- **Connected Security Solutions:** Smart locks, security cameras, and motion detectors provide real-time monitoring and peace of mind. Receive alerts when someone enters your home, lock or unlock doors remotely, and even have security cameras activate when motion is detected.

These are merely a few examples, and the smart home ecosystem continues to expand rapidly. Smart speakers that act as central hubs, voice-controlled assistants, and smart plugs that add intelligence to traditional appliances are all contributing to the symphony of a connected home.

3.2 Wearables: Transforming Wellness on Your Wrist

No longer just a watch, wearables are becoming sophisticated tools for monitoring our health and well-being. Here are some key wearables transforming the way we approach wellness:

- **Smartwatches:** These multifunctional devices offer features beyond just telling time. Track your heart rate, monitor your activity levels, receive notifications, and even make contactless payments with your smartwatch. Some smartwatches can also integrate with fitness trackers and health apps for a holistic view of your wellness.

- **Fitness Trackers:** Dedicated fitness trackers provide detailed insights into your daily activity. They can track steps taken, distance traveled, calories burned, and even sleep quality. This data can be used to set fitness goals, monitor progress, and make informed decisions about your health.

- **Health Monitoring Devices:** From smart scales that track weight and body composition to devices that monitor blood pressure or blood sugar levels, wearables are becoming increasingly sophisticated in the realm of health monitoring. These devices can empower individuals to take a proactive approach to managing chronic conditions or simply gain a deeper understanding of their overall health.

3.3 Smart Cities: Building the Future, Today

Imagine a city that adapts to its residents' needs in real-time. This is the vision of smart cities, where IoT empowers urban environments to become more efficient, sustainable, and citizen-centric. Here are some ways IoT is transforming cities:

- **Traffic Management:** Connected traffic lights and sensors optimize traffic flow, reducing congestion and travel times. Real-time data on traffic patterns can be used to adjust traffic light timings and inform drivers about alternative routes.
- **Infrastructure Monitoring:** Sensors embedded in bridges, buildings, and other infrastructure can detect potential problems before they occur. This enables proactive maintenance, preventing costly repairs and ensuring the safety of citizens.
- **Environmental Control:** Air quality sensors and smart meters can monitor energy consumption and environmental parameters. This data can be used to implement targeted initiatives to improve air quality, reduce energy waste, and create a more sustainable urban environment.
- **Citizen Services:** Smart parking solutions and waste management systems can be optimized using IoT.

Citizens can also access real-time information on public transportation, public safety alerts, and other essential services through connected platforms.

The concept of smart cities is still evolving, but the potential for IoT to improve urban living is immense. By harnessing the power of data and interconnected devices, cities can become more efficient, responsive, and ultimately, more livable.

3.4 Industrial Symphony: Revolutionizing Manufacturing with IoT

Factories are no longer just brick-and-mortar facilities; they are becoming intelligent ecosystems driven by IoT. Here's how IoT is transforming the industrial landscape:

- **Predictive Maintenance:** Sensors embedded in machinery can monitor performance and predict potential failures. This allows for proactive maintenance, preventing costly downtime and ensuring optimal production efficiency.

- **Asset Tracking:** Track the location and status of equipment, tools, and materials in real-time using RFID tags or other tracking solutions. This improves inventory management, optimizes resource utilization, and minimizes the risk of losing valuable assets.
- **Process Optimization:** IoT sensors can monitor various aspects of the production process, such as temperature, vibration, and energy consumption. This data can be used to identify inefficiencies, optimize production parameters, and improve overall quality control.
- **The Rise of Smart Factories:** By integrating various IoT technologies, factories are evolving into smart factories. These intelligent production facilities leverage real-time data to optimize processes, predict maintenance needs, and improve overall productivity and efficiency.

The impact of IoT in manufacturing extends beyond the

factory floor. Connected supply chains and logistics, enabled by real-time tracking and communication, are improving efficiency and streamlining product delivery. Additionally, connected products with embedded sensors can provide valuable insights into product performance and usage patterns, enabling data-driven product development and improved customer service.

The symphony of smart devices encompasses a wide range of applications, from transforming our homes and bodies to reshaping entire cities and industries. As technology continues to evolve and connectivity becomes even more pervasive, the possibilities for innovation and collaboration within the interconnected world of IoT are limitless.

CHAPTER 4

Unlocking the Power of IoT Data

The true magic of IoT lies not just in the interconnected devices themselves, but in the vast amount of data they generate.

4.1 Data Collection & Analytics: From Raw Data to Valuable Insights

The symphony of IoT devices produces a continuous stream of data. However, collecting and managing this data effectively is crucial. Here's a breakdown of the key steps:

- **Data Collection:** Strategies for data collection depend on the specific application and device capabilities. Sensors continuously collect data, which may be transmitted in real-time or at specific intervals. Gateways can aggregate data from various devices and send it to the cloud for further processing.

- **Data Filtering and Preprocessing:** Raw data from sensors may contain errors, inconsistencies, or irrelevant information. Data filtering techniques are used to clean the data and prepare it for analysis.

- **Data Storage:** Cloud platforms are a popular choice for storing large volumes of IoT data. However, depending on the sensitivity of the data or the need for real-time access, on-premise storage solutions or edge devices with local storage capabilities may also be utilized.

- **Data Analysis:** Once the data is clean and organized, it can be analyzed to extract meaningful insights. Techniques like statistical analysis, machine learning, and data mining can be used to identify trends, correlations, and patterns in the data.

The goal of data analysis in IoT is to transform raw data into actionable insights that can be used to:

- **Improve decision-making:** Data-driven insights can inform decisions about process optimization, resource allocation, and preventive maintenance in various contexts.

- **Gain operational efficiency:** By analyzing data on resource utilization and production processes, businesses can identify areas for improvement and streamline operations.

- **Develop new products and services:** Insights gleaned from user data and sensor information can inform the development of innovative products and services that cater to specific customer needs.

4.2 Big Data & Machine Learning: Supercharging Decision-Making

The vast amount of data generated by IoT devices falls under the umbrella of big data. Traditional data analysis methods may struggle to handle such large and complex datasets. Here's where big data technologies and machine learning come into play:

- **Big Data Analytics:** Big data platforms and tools are designed to handle the storage, processing, and analysis of massive datasets. These tools allow for faster and more efficient extraction of valuable insights from IoT data.

- **Machine Learning:** Machine learning algorithms can learn from historical data and identify patterns that may be difficult for humans to discern. This enables predictive analytics, allowing businesses to anticipate future trends, potential problems, and customer behavior.

By leveraging big data and machine learning, businesses can unlock the full potential of IoT data, gaining a deeper understanding of their operations, customers, and the surrounding environment. This empowers them to make data-driven decisions that are more informed, proactive, and ultimately, more successful.

4.3 Data Visualization: Transforming Numbers into Actionable Stories

Data on its own can be overwhelming and difficult to interpret. Data visualization plays a crucial role in transforming complex datasets into clear and compelling stories that effectively communicate insights to stakeholders. Here's why data visualization matters:

- **Improved Communication:** Visualizations like charts, graphs, and maps can simplify complex data, making it easier for audiences to understand trends and patterns.

- **Enhanced Decision-Making:** By presenting data visually, stakeholders can quickly identify key insights and make informed decisions based on the evidence presented.

- **Actionable Storytelling:** Effective data visualizations can tell a compelling story, highlighting opportunities, challenges, and areas requiring attention. This can motivate action and drive change based on the data analysis.

The choice of data visualization technique depends on the specific data and the message that needs to be communicated. Tools like dashboards, interactive visualizations, and real-time data displays can be used to create engaging and informative experiences for stakeholders.

4.4 Security & Privacy: Protecting the Data Symphony

With the growing importance of IoT data, concerns around security and privacy become paramount. Here's why securing the data pipeline is crucial:

- **Cybersecurity Threats:** IoT devices can be vulnerable to cyberattacks, potentially exposing sensitive data to unauthorized access. Strong security measures throughout the data collection, storage, and analysis process are essential.
- **Privacy Violations:** IoT devices collect personal data that needs to be handled responsibly. Clear data

governance policies and user consent mechanisms are crucial to ensure privacy is respected.

Security measures for IoT data include encryption, access controls, and regular security audits. Additionally, anonymizing data where possible and adhering to relevant data privacy regulations are crucial aspects of responsible data practices in the IoT ecosystem.

By implementing robust security measures and upholding strong privacy principles, organizations can ensure the data symphony of IoT remains secure and trustworthy. This fosters trust with users and stakeholders, paving the way for responsible innovation and the ethical use of data in the IoT world.

Data is the lifeblood of the Internet of Things. By collecting, analyzing, and visualizing this data effectively, organizations can unlock a wealth of insights that can transform their operations, products, and services. However, with great power comes great responsibility.

Securing the data pipeline and ensuring responsible data practices are fundamental aspects of building a sustainable and trustworthy IoT ecosystem. As we navigate the symphony of data generated by interconnected devices, it's crucial to find the right balance between innovation, security, and privacy to create a future where the power of IoT benefits everyone.

CHAPTER 5

IoT Revolutionizing Industries

The Internet of Things (IoT) is not just a technological trend; it's a transformative force reshaping entire industries.

5.1 Retail Revolution: Personalized Shopping Experiences

Imagine a shopping experience tailored to your individual needs and preferences. This is the future that IoT is enabling in the retail sector. Here are some ways IoT is revolutionizing retail:

- **Smart Shelves:** Inventory management gets a boost with smart shelves equipped with sensors. These shelves can track stock levels in real-time, automatically trigger reorders when necessary, and even display targeted promotions based on the products available.

- **Targeted Promotions:** IoT data on customer behavior can be used to deliver personalized promotions. Imagine receiving a discount on your favorite coffee brand as you walk by the coffee aisle, or recommendations for products based on your past purchases.

- **Enhanced Customer Experience:** Interactive displays, digital signage, and self-checkout kiosks powered by IoT can streamline the shopping experience, saving customers time and frustration.

- **Customer Behavior Analysis:** By analyzing data on customer traffic patterns and product interactions, retailers can gain valuable insights into customer preferences. This data can be used to optimize store layouts, improve product placement, and develop targeted marketing campaigns.

5.2 Cultivating the Future: Precision Farming with IoT

Agriculture is embracing the power of IoT to become more efficient, sustainable, and productive. Here's how:

- **Smart Irrigation Systems:** Soil moisture sensors and weather data analysis enable farmers to optimize irrigation practices. This reduces water waste, ensures crops receive the right amount of moisture, and ultimately improves crop yield.

- **Precision Fertilization:** Sensors can analyze soil composition and nutrient levels, allowing for targeted fertilization based on specific crop needs. This reduces fertilizer waste and ensures optimal nutrient delivery for healthy plant growth.

- **Livestock Monitoring:** Wearable sensors for livestock can track health status, location, and activity levels. This allows farmers to identify potential health problems early on, improve animal welfare, and optimize feeding schedules.

- **Weather Data Analysis:** Real-time weather data integrated with historical trends helps farmers make informed decisions about planting schedules, pest control, and crop protection measures.

5.3 Healthcare Transformed: Remote Patient Monitoring & Data-Driven Care

IoT is transforming healthcare by enabling remote patient monitoring and data-driven medical decisions. Here are some key aspects of this transformation:

- **Wearable Health Monitors:** Smartwatches, fitness trackers, and other wearables can track vital signs like heart rate, blood pressure, and sleep patterns. This data can be transmitted to healthcare providers remotely, allowing for early detection of potential health issues.

- **Telehealth Solutions:** Video consultations and remote monitoring platforms powered by IoT enable patients to receive medical care from the comfort of their homes. This improves access to healthcare services, especially for those in remote locations or with mobility limitations.

- **Data-Driven Diagnostics and Treatment:** The vast amount of health data collected through IoT devices can be analyzed to identify trends, predict potential health problems, and personalize treatment plans. This empowers healthcare professionals to make more informed decisions based on a wealth of patient data.

5.4 Transportation Evolved: Connected Vehicles for a Safer Journey

The future of transportation is connected. Here's how IoT is shaping the way we travel:

- **Self-Driving Cars:** Advanced sensor technology, real-time traffic data, and powerful computing capabilities are paving the way for autonomous vehicles. While still under development, self-driving cars have the potential to revolutionize transportation by improving safety, reducing traffic congestion, and increasing accessibility.
- **Traffic Management Systems:** Connected vehicles can communicate with traffic lights and

infrastructure, allowing for real-time traffic flow optimization. This reduces congestion, improves travel times, and contributes to a safer driving environment.

- **Predictive Maintenance for Vehicles:** Sensors embedded in vehicles can monitor engine performance, tire pressure, and other critical parameters. This data can be used for predictive maintenance, allowing for early detection and repair of potential problems, preventing breakdowns and ensuring vehicle safety.

- **Connected Transportation Ecosystems:** IoT is fostering the development of connected transportation ecosystems, which integrate various modes of transportation – cars, bikes, public transport – into a seamless network. This provides travelers with real-time information, journey planning options, and a more efficient overall experience.

These are just a few examples of how IoT is transforming industries. As technology continues to evolve and connectivity becomes even more pervasive, the possibilities for innovation and disruption across all sectors are limitless. The future belongs to those who can harness the power of IoT to create a more efficient, sustainable, and ultimately, a more connected world.

CHAPTER 6

Glimpsing the Future: Emerging Trends & Innovations

The world of IoT is constantly evolving, with new technologies and advancements emerging at a rapid pace.

6.1 Artificial Intelligence (AI) & IoT: A Match Made in Tech Heaven

The convergence of AI and IoT is a powerful combination. Here's why:

- **Intelligent Decision-Making:** AI algorithms can analyze the vast amounts of data generated by IoT devices, identify patterns, and make intelligent decisions in real-time. This can be applied in various contexts, from optimizing factory operations to predicting equipment failures in a proactive manner.
- **Automation on Steroids:** AI combined with IoT data can automate tasks and processes with greater

efficiency and accuracy. Imagine a self-driving car using real-time traffic data and sensor information to navigate roads autonomously, or a smart thermostat that learns your preferences and adjusts the temperature automatically.

- **Enhanced Analytics:** AI can analyze IoT data in real-time, enabling predictive analytics and proactive maintenance. This allows businesses to identify potential problems before they occur, minimizing downtime and optimizing resource utilization.

The synergy between AI and IoT has the potential to transform various industries, from manufacturing and transportation to healthcare and energy management. As AI algorithms become more sophisticated and data collection becomes even more pervasive, the possibilities for intelligent automation and data-driven decision-making will continue to grow.

6.2 Blockchain & IoT: Building Trust in a Connected World

Security and trust are paramount concerns in the interconnected world of IoT. Here's where blockchain technology comes in:

- **Enhanced Security:** Blockchain, with its decentralized and tamper-proof nature, can provide a secure platform for data exchange between IoT devices. This can be crucial for applications where sensitive data is involved, such as healthcare or financial transactions.
- **Improved Transparency:** Blockchain allows for transparent tracking of data provenance. This means users can be confident about the origin and authenticity of data collected by IoT devices.
- **Building Trust:** By establishing a secure and transparent data exchange ecosystem, blockchain can foster trust between different stakeholders within the IoT landscape. This can be particularly important

for applications involving multiple entities, such as connected supply chains or smart grids.

The integration of blockchain with IoT is still in its early stages, but it holds immense potential for building a more secure and trustworthy foundation for the future of the Internet of Things.

6.3 The Rise of Edge Computing: Processing Power Closer to the Source

Traditionally, data collected by IoT devices is transmitted to the cloud for processing. However, edge computing offers an alternative approach:

- **Decentralized Processing:** Edge computing involves processing data closer to the source, on devices like gateways or edge servers. This reduces latency (delay) in data processing, making it ideal for applications requiring real-time decisions or where internet connectivity may be limited.
- **Improved Efficiency:** By processing data at the

edge, less data needs to be transmitted to the cloud, which can save bandwidth and improve overall network efficiency.

- **Faster Response Times:** Real-time data processing at the edge enables faster response times for applications that require immediate action. Imagine a self-driving car needing to make split-second decisions based on sensor data, or a factory machine requiring real-time monitoring for potential malfunctions.

The rise of edge computing signifies a shift towards a more distributed processing architecture for the IoT ecosystem. This trend will likely continue as the need for real-time data processing and faster response times becomes increasingly important.

6.4 The Internet of Everything (IoE): Connecting Everything, Everywhere

The vision of the Internet of Things extends beyond just

connecting devices. The ultimate goal is to create an Internet of Everything (IoE) where everything, from devices and people to environments, is seamlessly interconnected and exchanging information:

- **Ubiquitous Connectivity:** Imagine a world where everything – from buildings and vehicles to wearables and environmental sensors – is connected and communicating with each other. This interconnectedness would create a vast network of data that can be used to gain insights, optimize processes, and ultimately, improve our lives.

- **Seamless Collaboration:** In an IoE world, devices, people, and environments can collaborate and share information to create a more intelligent and responsive world. Imagine a smart city where traffic lights adjust based on real-time traffic data and pedestrian crossings, or a smart home where your appliances automatically adjust to your needs and preferences.

The concept of IoE is still a futuristic vision, but the building blocks are already being put in place. As technology continues to evolve and connectivity becomes more pervasive, the potential for a truly interconnected world where everything communicates and collaborates becomes a closer reality.

The future of the Internet of Things is brimming with exciting possibilities. From the powerful synergy of AI and IoT to the secure and transparent data exchange facilitated by blockchain, and the distributed processing power of edge computing, the landscape is constantly evolving. As we move towards a future envisioned by the Internet of Everything (IoE), where everything is seamlessly connected and collaborating, the potential to improve our lives, optimize processes, and create a more intelligent and sustainable world is vast.

However, navigating this future also requires careful consideration of ethical implications, data privacy concerns, and the potential for digital divides. As we embrace the transformative power of IoT and its emerging trends, it's crucial to develop responsible practices and ensure equitable access to this transformative technology. By fostering collaboration, prioritizing security, and ensuring responsible data governance, we can unlock the true potential of the Internet of Things and build a future where interconnectedness empowers a better world for all.

CHAPTER 7

The Societal Impact of IoT

The Internet of Things (IoT) isn't just about technology; it's about its impact on society.

7.1 Smart Cities & Sustainable Living: Building a Greener Future

Cities are embracing IoT to become smarter and more sustainable. Here's how:

- **Environmental Monitoring:** Air quality sensors, noise pollution monitors, and smart water management systems can provide real-time data on environmental conditions. This data can be used to identify pollution sources, optimize resource usage, and implement targeted initiatives to create a more sustainable urban environment.
- **Resource Management:** Smart grids with

connected meters can optimize energy distribution and reduce consumption. Additionally, smart irrigation systems and leak detection sensors can conserve water resources.

- **Energy Efficiency:** Building automation systems that integrate with IoT sensors can optimize energy use in buildings, reducing overall energy consumption and greenhouse gas emissions. Imagine buildings that adjust lighting and temperature based on occupancy or real-time weather data.

By leveraging IoT for environmental monitoring and resource management, cities can pave the way for a greener future with a smaller environmental footprint.

7.2 Connected Communities & Improved Public Services

Beyond smart cities, IoT empowers communities to improve public services:

- **Enhanced Public Safety:** Connected security

cameras, smart lighting systems, and gunshot detection sensors can improve public safety and deter crime. Real-time data can also be used to deploy emergency services more efficiently.

- **Waste Management:** Smart waste bins with fill-level sensors can optimize waste collection routes and reduce unnecessary truck trips. This improves efficiency and reduces the environmental impact of waste management.

- **Infrastructure Optimization:** Sensors embedded in bridges, roads, and other infrastructure can detect potential problems before they occur. This allows for preventive maintenance, reducing repair costs, and improving public safety.

7.3 The Future of Work: Automation & The Changing Landscape

While automation powered by IoT can improve efficiency, it also raises concerns about job displacement. Here's how to navigate this change:

- **Skills Development:** As certain tasks become automated, the focus will shift towards skills like critical thinking, problem-solving, and creativity. Educational systems and workforce training programs need to adapt to equip individuals with the skills required in the evolving workplace.
- **Workforce Adaptation:** Upskilling and reskilling initiatives can help existing workers adapt to the changing job market. This will require collaboration between governments, educational institutions, and businesses to ensure a smooth transition.

The future of work will likely involve a more collaborative approach, where humans and intelligent machines work together to achieve optimal results.

7.4 Ethical Considerations: Privacy, Security, and Bias

The vast potential of IoT comes with ethical considerations that need to be addressed:

- **Data Privacy Concerns:** The vast amount of data

collected by IoT devices raises concerns about privacy. Clear data governance policies, user consent mechanisms, and robust security measures are crucial to protect user privacy and prevent misuse of data.

- **Security Risks:** As more devices become interconnected, the potential for cyberattacks increases. Implementing strong security protocols and addressing vulnerabilities throughout the IoT ecosystem is essential to ensure data security.

- **Bias in AI-powered Systems:** AI algorithms used in conjunction with IoT can perpetuate existing biases if not carefully designed and trained on diverse datasets. It's crucial to identify and mitigate potential biases in AI systems to ensure fair and ethical decision-making.

By proactively addressing these ethical considerations, we can ensure that the societal impact of IoT remains positive and promotes a future where technology empowers everyone.

The Internet of Things has the potential to transform our world in profound ways. From creating sustainable cities and improving public services to reshaping the workplace and fostering innovation across industries, the impact will be far-reaching. However, navigating this transformation requires a focus on responsible development, ethical considerations, and ensuring equitable access to the benefits of this transformative technology. By embracing the power of IoT responsibly, we can build a future where interconnectedness empowers a more sustainable, secure, and equitable world for all.

CHAPTER 8

Securing the Future of IoT

The vast potential of the Internet of Things (IoT) is undeniable. However, with great power comes great responsibility, especially when it comes to security.

8.1 Cybersecurity Threats in the IoT Landscape

The interconnected nature of IoT devices introduces unique security vulnerabilities that need to be addressed. Here's why securing the IoT landscape is crucial:

- **Large Attack Surface:** The sheer number of interconnected devices creates a vast attack surface for malicious actors. Exploiting vulnerabilities in a single device can provide a foothold for attackers to gain access to an entire network of devices.
- **Weak Security Protocols:** Many IoT devices are resource-constrained and may have limited

processing power. This can lead to them having weak security protocols, making them easier to hack.

- **Legacy Devices:** Many older IoT devices may not receive regular security updates, leaving them vulnerable to known exploits.

- **Data Breaches:** The vast amount of data collected by IoT devices, including potentially sensitive personal information, makes them attractive targets for cyberattacks. A data breach in an IoT ecosystem can have serious consequences for individuals and organizations alike.

8.2 Building Secure IoT Systems: Best Practices and Considerations

Securing the future of IoT requires a multi-pronged approach. Here are some key best practices:

- **Secure Device Development:** Security needs to be considered from the design stage onwards. This includes using strong encryption algorithms, implementing secure coding practices, and ensuring regular security updates are available for devices.

- **Network Protection:** Firewalls, intrusion detection systems, and other security measures need to be implemented to protect networks from unauthorized access and malicious activity.

- **Data Encryption:** Data collected by IoT devices, both at rest and in transit, needs to be encrypted to protect it from unauthorized access.

- **Authentication and Authorization:** Strong authentication and authorization mechanisms are essential to ensure only authorized devices and users can access the network and data.

- **Patch Management:** Regularly patching vulnerabilities in software and firmware is crucial to maintain a secure environment.

8.3 The Role of Regulations and Standards

Regulations and standards play a vital role in ensuring the security and privacy of the IoT ecosystem. Here's how:

- **Data Privacy Regulations:** Regulations like the General Data Protection Regulation (GDPR) and California Consumer Privacy Act (CCPA) mandate how organizations handle and protect personal data. These regulations apply to data collected by IoT devices as well.
- **Security Standards:** Standardization bodies are developing security standards for IoT devices. These standards provide a framework for manufacturers to follow when designing and developing secure devices.

8.4 Building a Culture of Cybersecurity

Security is not just about technology; it's also about people and processes. Here's how to foster a culture of cybersecurity:

- **Security Awareness Training:** Educating all stakeholders, from developers and manufacturers to users and administrators, about cybersecurity best practices is essential.

- **Security by Design:** Security needs to be integrated into the design and development of all IoT systems from the outset.

- **Shared Responsibility:** Security is a shared responsibility. Manufacturers, developers, network operators, and users all have a role to play in securing the IoT ecosystem.

Securing the future of IoT requires a collaborative effort from all stakeholders. By implementing best practices for secure device development, network protection, and data encryption, adhering to relevant regulations and standards, and fostering a culture of cybersecurity awareness, we can build a more secure and trustworthy foundation for the continued growth and innovation of the Internet of Things. As we embrace the transformative power of IoT, ensuring a secure future is not just an option; it's a necessity.

CHAPTER 9

THE ROAD AHEAD: CHALLENGES AND OPPORTUNITIES

The Internet of Things (IoT) holds immense promise for the future, but the road ahead is not without its challenges.

9.1 Interoperability and Standardization: Ensuring Compatibility

One of the biggest challenges in the IoT landscape is interoperability. Here's why it matters:

- **Fragmented Ecosystem:** Currently, there is a vast array of IoT devices and platforms from different vendors, many with proprietary protocols and communication standards. This lack of interoperability can make it difficult for devices from different manufacturers to work together seamlessly.

- **Data Silos:** Limited interoperability can lead to data

silos, where data collected by different devices remains isolated and cannot be easily integrated or analyzed. This hinders the potential for comprehensive insights and hinders the full potential of the IoT ecosystem.

- **Standardization Efforts:** Industry groups and regulatory bodies are actively developing standards for IoT devices and communication protocols. These standards aim to ensure compatibility between devices and platforms from different vendors, fostering a more unified IoT ecosystem.

Overcoming the challenge of interoperability is crucial for unlocking the full potential of IoT. As standardization efforts progress, we can expect a more unified and interoperable IoT landscape in the future.

9.2 Scalability and Sustainability: Managing Growth and Environmental Impact

The rapid growth of IoT devices presents both

opportunities and challenges:

- **Scalability Concerns:** Managing and scaling the vast amount of data generated by billions of interconnected devices requires robust infrastructure and efficient data management strategies.
- **Environmental Impact:** The production, use, and disposal of IoT devices can have an environmental impact. Sustainable manufacturing practices and responsible end-of-life management are crucial considerations.

Strategies for scalability include cloud-based data storage solutions with flexible scaling capabilities and the development of energy-efficient IoT devices. Additionally, promoting sustainable practices throughout the entire IoT lifecycle, from manufacturing to disposal, is essential.

9.3 The Digital Divide and Accessibility: Bridging the Gap

The benefits of IoT should not be limited to those with

access to technology. Here's why:

- **Digital Divide:** The gap between those who have access to technology and those who don't, the digital divide, can be exacerbated by the growth of IoT.
- **Ensuring Equitable Access:** It's crucial to develop strategies that ensure everyone can benefit from the advancements of IoT, regardless of socioeconomic background or location.

Bridging the digital divide requires initiatives like:

1. Affordable Technology: Developing and promoting affordable IoT devices and accessible data plans.
2. Digital Literacy Programs: Providing education and training programs to equip individuals with the skills needed to utilize IoT technologies effectively.
3. Inclusive Design: Designing IoT solutions that are accessible for people with disabilities.

9.4 The Future of Human-Machine Interaction: Collaboration and Co-evolution

As IoT continues to evolve, the way we interact with machines will change:

- **Natural User Interfaces:** Voice assistants, gesture recognition, and other natural user interfaces (NUI) will become increasingly common, facilitating more intuitive and natural interactions with IoT devices.
- **Collaborative Intelligence:** The future lies in humans and machines working together, with AI augmenting human capabilities and humans providing guidance and oversight to intelligent systems.
- **The Co-evolution of Humans and Machines:** As we interact more closely with intelligent machines, it's likely that both humans and machines will coevolve, adapting and learning from each other.

The future of human-machine interaction promises a world

where technology seamlessly integrates into our lives, empowering us to achieve more and create a better future.

The road ahead for IoT is paved with both challenges and opportunities. By addressing issues like interoperability, scalability, and the digital divide, while embracing sustainable practices and fostering a future of collaborative human-machine interaction, we can ensure that the Internet of Things fulfills its potential to create a more connected, sustainable, and equitable world for all. The future belongs to those who can harness the power of IoT responsibly and creatively, shaping a world where technology empowers us to live better, work smarter, and connect more deeply with the world around us.

CHAPTER 10

The Interconnected Future Awaits

10.1 A Recap: The Power and Potential of IoT

The Internet of Things (IoT) is not just a technological trend; it's a transformative force reshaping our world. This book has explored the vast potential of IoT, delving into its applications across various aspects of our lives. Here's a brief recap:

- **Smart Homes and Cities:** IoT is transforming our living spaces and urban environments into connected ecosystems, promoting efficiency, sustainability, and improved quality of life.
- **Revolutionized Industries:** From agriculture and manufacturing to healthcare and transportation, IoT is driving innovation and disruption across industries, optimizing processes and creating entirely

new possibilities.

- **Data-Driven Decision Making:** The vast amount of data generated by IoT devices empowers us to gain deeper insights, make data-driven decisions, and solve complex challenges in more effective ways.

- **A More Connected World:** IoT fosters a more interconnected world, where devices, people, and environments seamlessly communicate and collaborate, paving the way for a future of intelligent automation and a more integrated world.

10.2 A Call to Action: Embracing a Responsible Future

The potential of IoT is undeniable, but with great power comes great responsibility. As we embrace this transformative technology, it's crucial to prioritize responsible development and deployment:

- **Security and Privacy:** Robust security measures and strong data privacy practices are essential to ensure a safe and trustworthy IoT ecosystem.

- **Ethical Considerations:** We need to address ethical concerns surrounding data collection, bias in AI algorithms, and the potential for job displacement due to automation.
- **Sustainability:** Sustainable manufacturing practices, energy-efficient devices, and responsible end-of-life management are crucial for minimizing the environmental impact of IoT.
- **Digital Equity:** Bridging the digital divide and ensuring equitable access to the benefits of IoT for all is essential to create a truly inclusive future.

By prioritizing these aspects, we can ensure that the Internet of Things empowers humanity and fosters a positive impact on our world.

10.3 Looking Ahead: A Glimpse into the Evolving Landscape

The future of IoT is brimming with exciting possibilities. Here's a glimpse into what the evolving landscape might hold:

- **Ubiquitous Connectivity:** As technology advances, seamless connectivity will become even more pervasive, with everything from clothing and wearables to infrastructure and environmental sensors being interconnected.

- **Enhanced AI Integration:** Artificial intelligence (AI) will play an even greater role in the future of IoT, enabling smarter devices, more sophisticated automation, and real-time intelligent decision making.

- **The Rise of Ambient Intelligence:** The environment around us will become increasingly intelligent, with devices seamlessly integrated into our surroundings, anticipating our needs and responding proactively.

- **The Blurring Lines Between Physical and Digital:** The boundaries between the physical and digital world will continue to blur, creating a more immersive and interconnected reality.

These are just a few potential advancements on the horizon. The future of IoT is open-ended, and its possibilities are limited only by our imagination and creativity.

10.4 A Final Word: The Journey Begins Here

The world of IoT is vast and constantly evolving. This book has provided a foundation for understanding its potential and the considerations for responsible development. However, the journey doesn't end here.

We encourage you to:

- **Explore Further:** Delve deeper into specific areas of IoT that interest you. Research ongoing advancements, explore real-world applications, and stay informed about the latest trends.
- **Engage and Contribute:** Get involved in discussions about the future of IoT. Share your ideas,

contribute to responsible development practices, and help shape the future of this transformative technology.

- **Embrace the Possibilities:** The Internet of Things has the potential to revolutionize the way we live, work, and interact with the world around us. Be open to the possibilities, embrace innovation, and play a role in shaping a more connected and intelligent future for all.

The interconnected future awaits. Let's embark on this journey together, responsibly harnessing the power of IoT to create a better world.

ABOUT THE AUTHOR

Writer's Bio:

Benjamin Evans, a respected figure in the tech world, is known for his insightful commentary and analysis. With a strong educational background likely in fields such as computer science, engineering, or business, he brings a depth of knowledge to his discussions on emerging technologies and industry trends. Evans' knack for simplifying complex concepts, coupled with his innate curiosity and passion for innovation, has established him as a go-to source for understanding the dynamics of the digital landscape. Through articles, speeches, and social media, he shares his expertise and offers valuable insights into the impact of technology on society.

www.ingramcontent.com/pod-product-compliance
Lightning Source LLC
Chambersburg PA
CBHW050235230526
45470CB00005B/1956